Homemade Cakes, Cookies, and Tarts

Kari Finngaard

Homemade Cakes, Cookies, and Tarts

More Than 40 Traditional Recipes from Grandma's Kitchen to Yours

Translated by Madelaine Olsen

Skyhorse Publishing

Contents

Preface

Homemade sweets bring back memories from my childhood; they were special treats made by mom at home, my grandmother when visiting her, or during other special occasions. They were sweets made with love and care.

I will never forget mom's apple cake, baked with the season's juiciest Gravenstein apples—delicious apples native to southern Denmark—which she would spend several Saturday afternoons collecting in the fall.

A round cake tin filled with sugar cake dough, cinnamon, and apples found its way into the oven. The lovely smell of my mom's apple cake would soon fill the kitchen and the rest of the living room. A golden temptation turned into the highlight of the day, best accompanied by a slight scoop of cream.

Nor will I ever forget the dark chocolate cake I wished for at each of my birthday parties. A soft kind with bright yellow vanilla cream.

I can still remember the taste of the first bite as it melted in my mouth. Mom's sweets were neither complicated or particularly fancy. But they were good. And made by my mother.

A recent discovery of old recipes was my inspiration for this cookbook. Our grandmothers gathered friends and family in their living rooms over coffee tables filled with with pound cake, layer cake, and cookies. Recipes for cakes often live on for generations, and they're shared with friends and neighbors. It's important to keep traditional and tasteful classics alive. Some people choose to keep their family recipes secret and don't wish to share them with other people. However, I believe the opposite and I am more than happy to share my family recipes, that way other people can enjoy them as well.

It brings me such joy when a friend of mine calls to tell me that she successfully tried out one of my family recipes and asks for more she can try.

Baking should never become a duty or a project of prestige. You should bake because you want to bake. If the cake doesn't turn out as you had hoped, try again. Just as the saying goes, "practice makes perfect." The more you bake, the better you become at baking. Remember to spend some extra money on good quality ingredients, preferably organic ones from local producers.

Cakes don't have to look perfect. "Unsuccessful cakes are the best kind," a visiting friend of mine once told me. I had made a marble cake that had sunk in the middle. It didn't look very appetizing, but it was filled with butter, eggs, and chocolate so I made my best effort to make it look somewhat edible. As I put the tray of my miserable looking cake on the table I started excusing myself, "I must apologize, but . . ." Surprisingly, the cake disappeared in a matter of seconds.

Baking is like magic. There is something special happening every time we mix flour, sugar, and butter. While the cake is rising in the oven, the house smells like happiness. And cakes always taste better when they're shared with others.

Happy baking!

Kari Fringgaard

Lærebog

i de forskjellige Grene af

Husholdningen

af

Hanna Winsnes.

***

11te Udgave,
gjennemseet og forøget af Maren Winsnes.

***

Christiania.

I Kommission hos J. W. Cappelen.
Forlagt af Chr. A. Wulfsberg.

1880.

Baking
through the ages

Bread wasn't the only baked product back in ancient times. As early as the time of King David, cakes and other pastries were served. During the Viking Age, Norwegian Vikings got their taste of sweets in between their plundering. The Vikings brought the recipes with them back home and we know that cookies and other pastries were served in the homes of Norwegians by the twelfth century.

Honey was the only natural sweetener in baking before sugar, and it was heavily taxed. The world's oldest known honey is approximately from 1400 BC and can be found in two jars in a farming museum in Egypt. It is said that you can still eat the honey.

The wonderful smell of honey cakes filled with spices became popular, not only for their particularly good taste, but also because of how long they lasted. Honey had become such an important ingredient within baking that by the seventeenth century Norway's very own honey baking union was created. The union was created to protect the honey bakers' interests.

Up until the 1850s sugar was seen strictly as a medicine and was sold at a high price in pharmacies. It wasn't until people started to produce sugar in large quantities industrially that prices fell and regular people could afford the good, which had previously been regarded as a luxury product. Soon baking at home became more and more common within all classes of society. It became a tradition even for working class families to invite guests over for a cup of coffee, tea, or chocolate, and they competed in making the best and sweetest cakes.

Baking has become an important part of our food culture. In the eighteenth century millstones were increasingly used to produce fine, white flour. The mills were fundamental in the making of many fine cakes; served on special occasions such as holidays and parties in the homes of both the rich and poor. Cakes filled with cream and jam, many of them decorated with delicious berries and fruits.

By the nineteenth century the stove was common equipment in Norwegian homes and baking became more widespread. Today, people are still very keen on their childhood baking memories and continue to bake the same recipes over and over again.

Christmas baking is governed by traditions, how diligent we are, the amount of time we have, and the number of sweet tooths we have in the family. Most nations have a tradition of serving cookies during Christmas, but what's particular about the Norwegian tradition is to serve seven different kinds of cookies, all at once.

Back in the old days young ladies spent a lot of time preparing for marriage. They had to learn all the chores around the house. Mother and daughter baked together, discussed recipes, and argued over which ones to write down. Some of the first cook books were written in beautiful handwriting and can still be found well-preserved in museums.

Baking gives moments of happiness in the kitchen

Tools and ovens

 Back in the old days, women would use wooden spoons and hand mixers when they made the dough. Today, traditional baking tools have been replaced by electronic hand mixers and kitchen machines. Personally, I still prefer using the hand mixer when I bake cakes. It is simple to use and it covers almost all my needs. The hand mixer is particularly good when making Bundt cakes and sugar cakes.

Ovens can be tricky and they all function differently from each other; the temperature of one oven may be different from that of another oven. Because of the difference in ovens, your cakes might turn out too dark or too light in color. All the recipes in this book bake in a top and bottom heat conventional oven. You may also use a fan-based conventional oven. Explore the differences yourself.

My experience is that with a fan-based oven you need to put the temperature lower than the recipe indicates. It is important that you put the pastries in the oven when the red light has switched off; this means that the oven has reached its right temperature.

By putting Bundt cakes and sugar bread on a lower oven rack, you will get the best results. Roll cakes, choux pastry, cookies, and tarts should bake on the middle rack of the oven.

This is what you will need when you bake:

Scale and a measuring cup

Measuring spoons

Mixing bowl

Sieve

Rubber spatula and a wooden spoon

Hand mixer or food processor

Rolling pin

Cake tins

Pastry brush

Baking parchment

Measurements, weights, and abbreviations

Exact measurements are important in order to get successful results.

100 ML =

53 G ALL-PURPOSE FLOUR

85 G GRANULATED SUGAR

42 G POWDERED SUGAR

68 G POTATO FLOUR

40 G OATMEAL

60 G ALMONDS

140 G HONEY

36 G COCOA

ABBREVIATIONS

L = LITER

TBSP = TABLESPOON

TSP = TEASPOON

KG = KILOS

G = GRAMS

Ingredients

EGGS

- Eggs are an important part of the baking process. They help all the ingredients stick together to form a firm and smooth dough.
- One egg weighs approximately 60 grams.
- Use organic eggs; their yolks have a sunshine yellow color and they taste better. Using organic eggs will give you a golden result.
- The eggshell is a natural protector against bacillus and other bacteria. If the shield is broken, don't use the egg and throw it away instead.
- Eggs should be kept refrigerated, either in the egg carton or in the refrigerator's storage basket.
- Make sure the sharp end of the egg is facing down, this way the egg yolk is located in the middle of the egg white.
- Eggs should always be room temperature when you bake, therefore you should take the eggs out of the refrigerator a couple hours before you use them.

SUGAR

- Sugar, of course, makes cakes sweet and tasty. But sugar also contributes to creating a golden surface for your baked goods. If you successfully manage to calculate the right amount of sugar, the finished result will have a light, tender, and crumbly texture.
- We normally use white, granulated sugar with very fine sugar crystals when we bake. Alternatively you may also use brown cane sugar or demerara sugar. If you use the darker alternatives, your cakes might turn out a little more compact, but they will have a round and aromatic taste.
- Vanilla sugar is a regular baking additive in cakes. Powdered vanilla sugar should not contain fake ingredients. Preferably, you should use the seeds from a vanilla bean, especially when making vanilla cream and vanilla custard.
- Using Vanilla Extract instead of Vanilla Sugar: One teaspoon of vanilla extract is the equivalent of 1½ teaspoons of homemade vanilla sugar, or 1 teaspoon of commercially made vanilla sugar. Keep in mind that vanilla extract is not sweetened, so add an extra 1½ teaspoons of sugar per teaspoon of vanilla extract called for in the recipe.
- Icing sugar, or powdered sugar, is used to decorate baked goods; it can either be used as glaze or as powder dusted on top of finished cakes and desserts.

FATS

- Fat is an important ingredient in baking. It gives the dough a tender and moist texture.
- In my experience, the best type of fat is dairy butter, but margarine can be used as an alternative.
- A liquid fat such as vegetable oil is only used in a few particular recipes.

FLOUR

- All-purpose flour is used most frequently and fits almost all recipes. It binds other ingredients such as eggs and fats together to a dough.
- You should use good quality flour, and be aware of its expiration date.
- Measure flour with a light hand, that way you avoid lumps of flour in the batter. Using a sieve might be helpful.
- Store flour in an airtight container and keep it in a cool and dry place.

BAKING POWDER

- Baking powder causes the cakes to rise, and is primarily used in recipes for Bundt cakes, muffins, waffles, pancakes, and cookies.
- Baking powder should always be stored in an air tight container.
- Always make sure to mix baking powder and flour together before adding any other ingredients.

BAKING SODA

- Baking soda is a natural, white leavening agent, perfect for lighter cakes.
- 1 teaspoon of baking soda = 2 teaspoons of baking powder

BAKER'S AMMONIA

- Baker's Ammonia, or hartshorn, replaces baking powder as a leavening agent and is an old classic when it comes to old, traditional baking recipes. It is used frequently in traditional Norwegian baking, and can easily be found at supermarkets. Baker's ammonia can be purchased at most pharmacies, specialty stores, or online.

General baking tips

Before you start baking, read the recipe carefully.

Take all of your ingredients out of the fridge ahead of time before you start to bake, this way your ingredients get to the right room temperature.

Be patient.

Use fresh ingredients of good quality.

Use a measuring cup, preferably with a scale marked on the inside.

Always mix baking powder and flour together before adding any liquid ingredients.

When making sugar cakes, fill a cake pan three-quarters full, that way you leave enough room for the cake to rise as it bakes in the oven.

All cake pans must be buttered before adding dough. Use a pastry brush.

Most cakes and cookies are best the day they are baked.

Leave Bundt cakes in the Bundt pan and cover it with a layer of foil. If possible, keep the cake on the kitchen counter.

Bundt cake recipes are suitable for the freezer.

You may store cakes in the refrigerator, but make sure to take them out of the fridge ahead of time when you plan to serve it.

Never place hot cookies in a jar, wait instead until they have cooled down.

Do not put soft cakes and hard cakes together, keep them in separate boxes.

Classic
Bundt Cakes

Tips and advice for Bundt cakes

I will repeat it over and over. Remember to take ingredients such as eggs, butter, and milk out of the fridge ahead of time before you start baking. When all the ingredients are the same temperature, the recipe turns out the best. The dough becomes smooth and creamy, and you will be satisfied with the result.

Every so often, you will find a recipe that tells you to use chilled butter.

The kitchen should be nice and warm when you bake; all baked goods prefer rooms with a good temperature.

Whisk eggs and sugar until you get an airy and fluffy mixture.

Carefully mix flour and baking powder with the rest of the dry ingredients, preferably with a rubber spatula, that way the dough remains airy and soft.

You can use just about any type of pan when you bake Bundt cakes—bread pans, round cake pans, heart shaped cake pans, and triangle shaped cake pans.

The pan should be filled about three-quarters full with batter, to leave enough space for the cake to rise while baking.

To avoid the dough getting stuck to the sides of the pan, grease the pan prior to baking. Using a pastry brush will aid you in reaching all corners, not leaving any uncoated shiny spots.

Do not open the door of your oven too early. You can cause your cake to crack or collapse.

To test if the cake is done, use a thin item (such as a toothpick, thin butter knife, etc.) to poke the cake in the middle. If the item comes up with some wet batter, the cake needs to bake some more. It is important that the cake does not bake for too long; you want to avoid a dry cake.

Let the cake rest for a few minutes before you remove it from the pan. Cool the cake on a drying rack, so that excess moisture will evaporate.

Marble cake

A classic we never get tired of. It is also called tiger cake.

1 cup (200g) butter, room temperature

1 cup (250ml) sugar

3 eggs

1½ (350ml) cup all-purpose flour

1½ tsp baking soda

1 tsp vanilla-flavored sugar

2 tbsp cocoa powder

Preheat oven to 350°F (175°C).
Mix butter and sugar until you have an airy and smooth mixture.
Add eggs, one at a time.
In a separate bowl, mix flour and baking soda.
Carefully add the egg mixture into the flour bowl.
Pour one-third of the mixture into a separate bowl.
Add cocoa and vanilla-flavored sugar to the rest of the mixture.
Pour half of the light mixture into a buttered loaf pan (pan should be approximately the size of
    6½ cups water).
Pour the cocoa mixture over the light mixture in the pan, then pour the rest of the light mixture over
    the cocoa.
Carefully draw a fork through all three layers.
Bake in the middle of the oven for 45–50 minutes.
Let the cake rest in the pan for a few minutes.
Cool the cake on a wire rack.

Tips

Adding a few drops of lemon will give your cake a fresh taste.

Spice Cake

A cake with a taste of childhood. The spices in this cake keep your entire house smelling like Christmas all year round.

½ cup (100g) butter

1 ¼ cup (300ml) sugar

1 ¼ cup (300ml) all-purpose flour

2 tsp ground cardamom

1 tsp ground cinnamon

1 tsp ground cloves

2 tsp baking powder

2 eggs

3⅓ ounces (100ml) cream

Preheat oven to 350°F (175°C).
Melt the butter, then cool down to just above room temperature.
Mix butter and sugar until you have an airy and smooth mixture.
Blend all dry ingredients.
Mix eggs, cream, and the butter/sugar mixture together.
Blend all the ingredients thoroughly until you have a soft and smooth batter.
Pour the batter into a buttered cake pan (pan should be approximately the size of 6½ cups).
It is important that you fill three-quarters of the pan.
Bake in the middle of the oven for 35 minutes.
Let the cake rest in the pan for a few minutes before you cool it on a wire rack.

Tips
Adding more spices will enhance the taste.
Remember that all ovens work differently.
Pay careful attention the last minutes of baking.

Tosca cake

A golden and moist cake that keeps well. A favorite on all dessert tables.

CAKE LAYER:

½ cup (100g) butter

1 cup (200ml) sugar

3 eggs

1 cup + 3 tbsp (250ml) all-purpose flour

½ tsp baking powder

TOPPING:

½ cup (100ml) chopped almonds

⅓ cup (75 ml) sugar

⅓ cup (75g) butter

1 tbsp all-purpose flour

1 tbsp milk

Preheat oven to 350°F (175°C).

Melt the butter; cool down to just above room temperature.

Whisk sugar and eggs until you get an airy mixture.

Add butter.

In a separate bowl, mix flour and baking powder.

Blend the dry and the wet mixtures together.

Pour the batter into a buttered, round cake pan (approximately 9½ inches).

Bake the cake layer for 25–30 minutes.

Mix all of the topping ingredients together in a pot.

Carefully heat up the mixture, but be careful to not let it boil.

Take the cake out of the oven, cover the top with the topping mixture.

Put the cake back in the oven and bake for another 15 minutes.

The cake should have a golden caramel color.

Let the cake cool.

Tips

Store the cake in an airtight container, or a plastic bag. That way it will remain fresh.

Tosca cake is suitable for freezing.

Chocolate cake

As a child, chocolate cake was my favorite pick at all birthday celebrations.
My mom would always serve it with a scoop of thick vanilla cream.

⅔ cup (150g) butter

1¼ cup (300ml) sugar

1 cup (250ml) all-purpose flour

2 tsp baking powder

1 tsp vanilla sugar

3 tbsp cocoa powder

2 eggs

½ cup (100ml) warm water

Powdered sugar for cake decorating

Preheat oven to 350°F (175°C).
Melt the butter, allowing it to cool to just above room temperature.
Blend all the dry ingredients together in a bowl.
Add butter.
Add eggs, one at a time.
Add the warm water last.
Pour the batter into a round, buttered cake pan (approximately 9½ inches).
Bake on the middle rack of your oven for 40 minutes.
Let the cake cool.
Sprinkle powdered sugar over the cake as you are ready to serve.
Best accompanied by homemade vanilla cream; find the recipe on page 133.

Tips

An old-fashioned housewife-tip is to add some warm water to the batter.
This will make the cake moist.
Cocoa powder is nice to use as an additive in soft cakes and desserts.
Cocoa powder contains 25 percent less fat than chocolate, and is therefore suitable for recipes that have a lot of fat.

Classic sugar cake

The cake we have baked through generations.
Perfect for all occasions.

⅓ cup (75g) butter

2 eggs

1 cup (200ml) sugar

1¼ cup (300ml) all-purpose flour

1½ tsp baking powder

1 tsp vanilla sugar

⅔ cup (150ml) boiling water

Preheat oven to 350°F (175°C).

Melt the butter, and allow it to cool down to just above room
temperature.

Whisk sugar and eggs until you get an airy mixture.

Add butter.

In a separate bowl, mix flour, baking powder, and vanilla
sugar.

Blend the dry mixture with the wet mixture.

Add the boiling water.

Pour the batter into a buttered, round cake pan (should be
approximately the size of 6½ cups).

Bake for 40 minutes.

Let the cake rest for a few minutes before you remove it from
the pan.

Cool the cake on a wire rack.

Some facts about the classic sugar cake

I would dare to assert that the classic sugar cake is the traditional cake of the neighboring

country of my homeland, Sweden.

Swedes have baked sugar cakes for ages, and there are several different recipes.

Originally, one would use whatever ingredients one could find in the kitchen, most importantly eggs,

sugar, butter, and flour.

The more eggs added to the batter, the better the cake would be.

Sugar cakes are soft and moist, and they can be stored over time and still taste good.

They are suitable for freezing.

Sugar cakes typically bake in Bundt pans.

Sugar cakes taste good alone, but there are multiple variations. You may add lemon zest, a few drops of

orange, some vanilla sugar, or chopped chocolate to the recipe. Take your pick.

You can also cover the cake with melted chocolate.

Fresh fruits and berries are good alternatives.

Sugar cake pans with old-fashioned shapes create nostalgia in the kitchen. If you are not lucky enough to

have inherited old pans, take a look at local flea markets or antique stores.

Sugar cake with a taste of lemon

The lemon zest gives this cake a fresh, acidic taste.

¼ cup (50g) butter

2 eggs

1 cup (200ml) sugar

½ cup (100ml) milk

1 ¼ cup (300ml) all-purpose flour

2 tsp baking powder

1 tsp lemon zest

Preheat oven to 350°F (175°C).
Melt the butter, cool down to just above room temperature.
Whisk sugar and eggs until you get an airy mixture.
Add milk and butter.
In a separate bowl, mix flour and baking powder.
Carefully blend the dry mixture with the wet mixture.
Add lemon zest.
Pour the batter into a buttered Bundt pan (should be
    approximately the size of 6½ cups).
Bake on the lower rack in oven for 40 minutes.
Let the cake rest for a few minutes before you remove it from
    the pan.
Cool the cake on a wire rack.

Sugar cake with spices and apples

An exciting twist, where slices of apples and spices give a little extra flavor.

⅓ cup (80g) butter

1 cup (200ml) sugar

3 eggs

1½ cups (300ml) all-purpose flour

1½ tsp baking powder

1 tsp ground cinnamon

½ tsp ground cardamom

½ cup (100ml) warm water

1 apple

Preheat oven to 350°F (175°C).
Melt the butter, and allow it to cool down to just above room temperature.
Whisk sugar and eggs until you get an airy mixture.
Blend butter with the mixture.
In a separate bowl, mix flour, baking powder, and spices.
Blend the dry mix with the airy mixture.
Add warm water.
Pour the batter into a buttered, loaf-shaped pan (pan should be approximately the size
    of 6½ cups).
Remove the core of the apple, but keep the skin around the apple.
Cut the apple in rings and then slice them in two.
Spread the apples over the cake batter.
Bake on the lower rack in oven for 50–55 minutes.
Let the cake rest for a few minutes before you remove it from the pan.
Cool the cake on a wire rack.

Tips

This moist cake holds up well for a couple of days on the kitchen counter, and a few more days if kept in the fridge.
The sugar cake is also suitable for freezing.
When the cake has cooled down (and there are still a few pieces left after day one), I like to keep the cake in the Bundt pan, cover it with a plastic bag, and store it in the fridge.

Cakes with Fruit and Berries

Seasonal baking

We live in a fast-paced world. Our meal choices are often based on how quick and easy they are to prepare, and we frequently resort to fast food. There is not enough time for your weekly chores to fit into your schedule.

It is impossible to escape time. But a homemade dinner made from scratch, or a freshly baked cake coming straight from the oven are still tempting.

Occasionally we should set aside a few extra hours and make real food, prepared with love and care. It is all about priorities.

Back in the days of our grandparents, seasonal food was all the rage. Particularly on the country side. Mother hen laid her eggs all year round. The seasons would then decide what people ate, and it was a matter of exploiting all the resources in gardens, woods, and the yields.

In the spring, both the young and old would plant crowns of rhubarb. Vegetables from the garden and berries from the woods would keep the housewife busy during the summer seasons. When fall was around the corner one would pick fruits from trees or go mushroom hunting in the deepest woods. A full basket was a valuable supply for the kitchen.

The results were jam, marmalade, and fruit jars.

A well-stocked larder was important for a long winter.

Some of my grandmother's customs are worth keeping alive.

How about surprising someone special with a basket filled with blueberries, or a freshly baked cake? Or decorate the your little one's birthday cake with blushing raspberries? Apple cake with cinnamon can tempt anyone during the fall. Because there is nothing like homemade food. And it does not need to take that much time.

Swiss roll with raspberry jam

A classic quick cake—sweet and sinful. In my house, we filled the Swiss roll with raspberry jam. But you may vary the filling with what you have and like.

3 eggs

⅔ cup (150ml) sugar

2 tbsp milk

1 cup (200ml) all-purpose flour

1 tbsp baking powder

Sugar and raspberry jam

Preheat oven to 440°F (225°C).
Whisk sugar and eggs until you get an airy mixture.
Add milk to the mixture.
In a separate bowl, mix flour and baking powder.
Carefully add the flour mix to the airy mixture, using a spatula.
Spread the batter evenly over a parchment paper-lined sheet pan; the spatula is excellent to use here as well.
Bake on the middle rack in oven for 7–8 minutes.
Sprinkle sugar over a second piece of greaseproof paper.
When done, turn the finished cake over and place it on the sugared paper.
Carefully remove the greaseproof paper that is now on top of the cake (start from the bottom and work your way up).
While the cake is still warm, spread a layer of jam evenly across the cake.
Roll the cake.
Place the Swiss roll with its joint faced down.
Let it cool before cutting slices.

Swiss roll tips

The cake batter should be evenly smoothed out to all edges of the greaseproof paper, using a spatula.
Do not bake for too long, or it will be trickier to roll.
Quickly remove the cake from the oven. It is then perfectly moist and elastic, and is easier to roll.
When you use jam as filling, it is not necessary to cool the cake layer.
Before serving, cool the cake with its seam faced down.
You may fill Swiss rolls with jam, applesauce, cream, or chocolate cream.
On page 134, you will find a simple recipe for chocolate cream.

Raspberry gateau with custard

The perfect birthday cake. Or an eye catching piece for your summer party when placed on a dessert table.

1 cup (200ml) sugar

3 eggs

1 ¼ cup (300ml) all-purpose flour

2 tsp baking powder

½ tsp vanilla sugar

4 cups (500g) raspberries

½ cup (50g) sliced almonds

¼ cup (50g) refrigerated butter

Preheat oven to 355°F (180°C).
Whisk sugar and eggs until you get an airy mixture.
In a separate bowl, mix flour, baking powder, and vanilla sugar.
Blend the dry mix with the wet mixture.
Gently blend in half of the raspberries.
Pour the batter into a buttered Bundt pan (approximately the size of
    6½ cups).
Evenly sprinkle sliced almonds over the top of the cake, then cut
    the butter and sprinkle this evenly as well.
Bake on the middle rack in oven for approximately 30 minutes.
Let the cake cool.
Decorate the cake with the rest of the raspberries.
The cake tastes extra good when served with homemade custard
(you can find the recipe on page 133).

Tips

Remember to bake with fresh berries.
Carefully wash the berries to avoid having rotten berries that disrupt the taste.

Raspberry cookies

Easy to bake, sweet temptations with raspberry jam.

40–45 COOKIES

⅔ cup (150g) refrigerated butter

¼ cup sugar (50ml) sugar

1 ¼ cup (300ml) all-purpose flour

¼ cup (50ml) potato starch

1 tbsp cold water

Raspberry jam

Preheat oven to 390°F (200°C).
Cut the butter into small cubes.
Stir butter and sugar in a bowl.
With your fingers, gather and press the mixture into a batter.
Add water, flour, and potato starch.
Stir until you have a smooth and soft dough.
Divide the dough into halves; roll out each half into lengths.
Cut each length into approximately 20 pieces.
Roll the pieces into small balls and put them on a greaseproof
    baking paper.
Lightly press your finger in the middle of each cookie.
Put raspberry jam on top of each cookie.
Bake on the middle rack of oven for approximately 15 minutes.
Let the cookies cool.

Tip

You may replace raspberry jam with other sorts of jam,
blueberry for example.

Blueberry tart with lattice

A good, traditional cake bringing back good memories from summer vacations spent as a child.

TART DOUGH:

2¾ cup (350g) all-purpose flour

½ tsp baking powder

¾ cup (170g) cold butter, cut in cubes

½ cup (115g) sugar

1 egg

FILLING:

4 ¼ cups (1l) blueberries

4 tbsp sugar

1 tsp vanilla sugar

Mix flour and baking powder in a bowl.
Add butter.
With your fingers, gather and press the mixture into a batter.
Add sugar.
Whisk the egg first, then mix it with the batter.
Roll two-thirds of the dough, using a rolling pin.
Press the dough into a round tart pan (approximately 26 inches).
Tap the dough, using a fork.
Store the tart dough in the fridge for approximately 30 minutes.
Preheat oven to 375°F (190°C).
Evenly, sprinkle blueberries over the tart-shell.
Sprinkle sugar and vanilla sugar as well.
Roll out the rest of the dough.
Cut the dough into thin strips.
Place the lengths across the tart in a lattice.
Bake in oven for approximately 40 minutes.
Let the tart cool.

Tips

Serve the cake alone, or with whipped cream sweetened with vanilla sugar.
In this recipe, you may also use raspberries, blackberries, or slices of apple.

Norwegian pancakes with blueberries

The children's favorite. In the late summer we go berry-picking. The harvest usually becomes fresh blueberry jam we put on pancakes or slices of bread. In the winter time, blueberry jam is our favorite. These are a bit thinner than your typical pancakes and are more similar to crepes, but are delicious nonetheless.

MIXTURE FOR 10–12 PANCAKES

2 tbsp butter, melted

2 eggs

1¼ cup (300ml) milk

1 cup (250ml) all-purpose flour

1 tsp baking powder

2 tbsp sugar

Decoration: Blueberries and powdered sugar

Mix melted butter with eggs and half of the milk.

In a separate bowl, mix flour, baking powder, and sugar.

Add the dry mixture to the wet mixture and whisk until you have a smooth mixture.

Blend in the other half of milk.

Melt butter in a frying pan.

Cook small pancakes on middle-heat.

Cook for a few minutes on each side until you see a golden color.

Serve with blueberries and powdered sugar on top.

INTERNATIONAL PANCAKE DAY

International Pancake Day takes place on the Tuesday before Ash Wednesday. In my home country of Norway, we celebrate by eating pancakes after the *Fastelavn* Carnival, which happens the Monday or Sunday before Pancake Day.

People celebrate this day in different ways across the world; some have carnivals, others arrange pancake marathons. According to old customs, Christians had to fast 40 days prior to Easter. Because of this, families had to get rid of groceries such as eggs, milk, sugar, and all-purpose flour. In France, the day is called *Mardi Gras*, which means *Fat Tuesday*.

Crumble tart
with rhubarb

*Crumble tart tastes wonderful when served with coffee,
and as dessert. Oatmeal provides extra flavor.*

1 ¼ lb (500g) fresh stalks of rhubarb

½ cup (100g) brown sugar

¾ cup + 1 tbsp (100g) all-purpose flour

½ cup (100g) butter

½ cup (100g) oatmeal

1 tsp vanilla sugar

½ cup (50g) sliced almonds

Preheat oven to 355°F (180°C)
Wash the rhubarb and cut into 1-inch pieces.
Put rhubarb and sugar in a sauce pan.
Boil for 5 minutes.
Put rhubarb in a buttered pan (approximately 10 inches).
Crumble butter and flour, using your hands.
Stir in oatmeal, vanilla sugar, and almond flakes.
Evenly pour the mixture over the rhubarb.
Bake in oven for approximately 40 minutes.
Let the tart cool.

Tips

Crumble tarts can be made in an endless number of variations,
with both berries and fruits.
You may substitute rhubarb with slices of apples or pears, for
example. If you decide to do so, you place the slices directly into
a buttered pan.
Crumble tart tastes extra good when served with whipped cream
or ice cream.

Apple pie

Apple pie is one of my favorites, especially during the time of year when the trees are bursting with fruits. Keep the skin on the apples; it gives the cake a beautiful, rustic look.

1⅔ cup (200g) all-purpose flour

1½ teaspoons baking powder

½ cup (100g) sugar

¾ cup (150g) butter, softened

3–4 apples

Pearl sugar (This can be purchased at most specialty
   food stores or made at home.)

Preheat oven to 390°F (200°C).
Blend flour and baking powder in a mixing bowl. Add sugar.
Add butter, and crumble the ingredients using your fingers.
Add eggs, one at the time.
Mix the ingredients gently in a circular motion.
Remove the core of the apples, but keep the skin on.
Slice the apples into wedges.
Evenly roll out the dough in a buttered Bundt pan
   (approximately 9½ inches).
Nicely arrange the apples in the dough (have a look at the
   picture).
Sprinkle with pearl sugar.
Bake in the middle of the oven for approximately 30 minutes.
Let the pie cool.

Tips

Apple pie tastes especially good when accompanied with whipped cream or ice cream.
You can find my homemade vanilla ice cream recipe on page 133.
You may sprinkle almond slices over the pie before you put it in the oven.

Glazed apple tart

A cake of French origin. A warm apricot jam glaze gives the tart a beautiful, golden look.

TART DOUGH:

2½ cups (300g) all-purpose flour

1 cup (100g) powdered sugar

1 cup (200g) cold butter, cut in cubes

1 egg yolk

2 tbsp cold water

FILLING:

4 sour apples

4–5 tbsp apricot jam

1 tsp lemon juice

Crumble flour, powdered sugar, water, and butter, using your hands.
Whisk in the egg yolk.
Shape the dough so you have a lump, and wrap it in plastic wrap.
Place the dough in a fridge and leave it in for at least an hour.
Preheat oven to 375°F (190°C).
Roll the dough on a floured surface.
Press the dough gently on a buttered Bundt pan (approximately 11 inches).
Make sure the dough covers all edges.
Remove the core of the apples, and cut the apples into thin slices.
Cover the tart dough with apple slices.
Bake in oven for 25–30 minutes.
Heat up apricot jam and lemon juice in a small sauce pan.
Brush the apples with the warm mixture.
Serve the apple tart with vanilla cream; you can find the recipe on page 133.

Tips

Peeled apples often turn brown. To prevent discoloration, pour a few drops of lemon juice over the apples.

Apple and pear tart

Seasonal food was part of my grandmother's kitchen. Use seasonal fruits in a cake with an elegant, country western look.

TART DOUGH:

2 cups (250g) all-purpose flour

⅔ cup (125g) cold butter, cut in cubes

2 tbsp sugar

1 egg

3 tbsp cold water

FILLING:

2 apples

2 pears

2 tbsp (25g) butter

3–4 tbsp sugar

Sliced almonds

Using your hands, rub flour and butter together in a bowl.

Keep rubbing with your fingertips, until you have a smooth batter.

Add sugar and a whipped egg.

Add cold water; blend gently until you have a dough.

Roll the dough to a circular shape on a floured surface.

Place the dough in a buttered Bundt pan (approximately 10 inches).

Make sure the dough extends approximately 1 inch outside the pan's edges.

Preheat oven to 390°F (200°C)

Remove the core of the apples and the pears.

Cut the fruit into small pieces.

Spread the fruit over the tart dough.

Sprinkle with sugar, small chunks of butter, and almond flakes.

Fold and roll the top edge under lower edge.

Bake on the middle rack of the oven for 45–50 minutes.

Let the tart cool.

Tips

Cinnamon gives the apple and pear tart extra flavor.

You may replace apples and pears with blueberries and raspberries.

Pear cake with a taste of almonds

A moist family-cake. A classic sugar cake base, pears, spices, and almonds give this cake an entirely new tasting experience.

¼ cup (50g) butter

2 fresh pears

1 tbsp cornstarch

1 egg

½ cup (100ml) sugar

½ cup (100ml) milk

⅔ cup (150ml) all-purpose flour

2 tsp baking powder

1 tsp ground cinnamon

1 tsp cardamom

¼ cup (50g) sliced almonds

powdered sugar for decoration

Preheat oven to 350°F (175°C).
Melt butter, and let it cool for a couple minutes.
Wash the pears, keep the skin on.
Remove the core of the pears, slice up into cubes.
Sprinkle cornstarch over pears.
Whisk eggs and sugar into an airy mixture.
Blend butter and milk into the mixture.
In a separate bowl, mix flour and baking powder, add spices.
Blend the flour mix and the wet mixture together.
Finally, add pear cubes and almond flakes to the mixture.
Pour the mixture into a buttered Bundt pan (pan should be the size of approximately 6½ cups).
Bake in oven for 40 minutes.
Let the tart cool.
Sprinkle powdered sugar over the cake before serving.

Tips

You may serve the tart with hot chocolate sauce. You can find the recipe on page 134.

Fruit cake

This is a typical Christmas cake. Personally, I think the cake tastes just as good when summer arrives.

3½ ounces (100g) dried apricots

3½ ounces (100g) prunes

2½ ounces (75g) raisins

¼ cup (50ml) squeezed orange juice or calvados

⅔ cup (150g) softened butter

1 cup (200ml) sugar

4 eggs

2 cup (250g) all-purpose flour

1 tsp baking powder

Cut apricot and prunes into small pieces.
Put raisins and fruit in a cup; pour orange juice or calvados over the dried fruit.
Leave it in the cup for about half an hour.
Preheat oven to 350°F (175°C).
Whisk butter and sugar into an airy mixture.
Add eggs, one at the time.
In a separate bowl, mix flour and baking powder.
Mix all of the ingredients together until you have a dough. Add the fruit mixture.
Pour the mixture into a buttered bread pan.
Bake in oven for 50–60 minutes.
Cover the cake with foil the last 10 minutes of baking if it looks too dark.
Let the cake cool.

Tips

Cover the cake with plastic wrap when you store it. It pulls all the flavors together that way, and as time goes by the cake will actually taste better.
If you store the cake in the fridge, it will still taste good after several weeks.

Traditional Cakes

Traditional baking

Family and a sense of belonging are fundamental needs to us all. We should cherish our family traditions and let our dearest childhood memories live on. What we learned or ate at our parents' or grandparents' homes have left lasting impressions on our taste buds.

Sveler, a batter cake, similar to pancakes in consistency, is a traditional dessert that usually accompanies a cup of coffee in Western Norway, especially in the county *Møre og Romsdal*. My grandparents lived in Kristiansund, a city that was a whole eternity away from the big capital for a little girl. When summer finally arrived and my summer break began, I was at my happiest; I knew it was time for our yearly visit to my mom's birth town.

A train, a bus, and a ferry—the trip seemed like an endless expedition. When we arrived, the entire family was reunited for a cup of coffee.

I have a slight memory of my grandmother's smile, a freshly ironed table cloth with cross stitches, and her flower-decorated porcelain tableware.

A table crammed with delicious homemade cakes tempted a hungry child's stomach. The *sveler* was a natural part of the dessert table. They had a heavenly smell, served with butter and brunost, a type of caramelized Scandinavian whey cheese similar to *dulce de leche*, folded along the middle.

I also remember my grandfather's daily coffee ritual. As an ending to the meal, he would pour some coffee on his plate, dip a cube of sugar in it, and just enjoy his last sip.

Recipes for *sveler* vary from village to village. Back in the day, there was also a difference of the types of *sveler* you would serve at the coffee table and at special occasions.

Sveler

Sveler is a Norwegian cake that looks similar to the American pancake, but is usually eaten with afternoon coffee. Sveler is often served with fresh raspberry jam. You can also eat sveler with brunost, sour cream, or vanilla cream.

12 PIECES

2 eggs

½ cup (100ml) sugar

1 ½ cups (300ml) buttermilk

2 cups (400ml) all-purpose flour

½ tsp baking soda

½ tsp baker's ammonia

2 tbsp melted butter

Whisk eggs and sugar.
Add buttermilk.
In a separate bowl, mix flour, baking soda, and baker's ammonia.
Gently add the flour mixture to the egg mixture, using a sieve will prevent the creation of lumps.
Whisk until you have a smooth mixture.
Add butter at the end.
Heat a pan or a griddle on medium temperature.
Use a ladle and pour a small amount of batter on the heated pan.
Cook the sveler on both sides.
Let cool before serving.

Some facts about sveler

Sveler look like pancakes and are approximately ½ inch (1cm) thick and 6 inches (15cm) in diameter.
Sveler consists of sugar, eggs, flour, buttermilk, baking soda, baker's ammonia, and butter. If you replace sugar with salt, you will get a Russian variety of sveler, called blinis.
Back in the day, sveler was made on griddles, but most people use regular pans today.

Banana cake

Banana cake is an old classic, and one of the first cakes I learned how to bake in the school kitchen. It is most common to make banana cake without nuts, but my experiment using walnuts yielded great results. You may also use hazelnut kernels.

½ cup (100g) soft butter

½ cup (100ml) sugar

2 eggs

2 ripe bananas

1½ cup (200ml) all-purpose flour

1 tsp baking powder

1 tsp vanilla sugar

½ cup (50g) walnut kernels, coarsely chopped

Preheat oven to 350°F (175°C).
Whisk butter and sugar to a light and porous mixture.
Add eggs, one at the time.
Mash the bananas, using a fork.
Blend the banana with the egg mixture.
In a separate bowl, mix flour and baking soda.
Add vanilla sugar and walnuts.
Blend all the ingredients together until you have a smooth dough.
Pour the dough into a buttered bread pan (approximately 4⅓ cups in size).
Bake in oven for 45–50 minutes.
Let the cake rest in the pan for a few minutes.
Cool the cake on a wire rack.

Tips

Do not throw away ripe bananas. They are ideal in this recipe. The riper they are, the easier it is to mash them.
Place a piece of foil or greaseproof paper over the pan if the cake looks too dark towards the end of the baking time.
Insert a thin wooden stick in the middle of the cake to make sure it is done baking.

Choux pastry

Airy cakes with vanilla cream and powdered sugar.

12 PIECES

1 cup (250ml) water

⅓ cup (75g) butter

¼ tsp (1ml) salt

1 tsp sugar

1 ¼ cup (150g) all-purpose flour

4 eggs

powdered sugar for decoration

VANILLA CREAM:

1 ¼ cup (300ml) heavy cream

1 tsp vanilla sugar

1 tsp sugar

Preheat oven to 410°F (210°C).
Boil water, butter, salt, and sugar in a sauce pan.
Sprinkle flour into the mixture.
Stir vigorously with a wooden spoon until the dough lets go of the bottom of the pan.
Remove the pan from the heated plate.
Add eggs, one at a time.
Stir well until you have a smooth dough.
Shape the choux pastry with the help of two tablespoons.
Place them on a greaseproof paper.
Make sure there's plenty of space between cookies!

Bake in oven for 25–30 minutes; do not open the oven door during this time.
Cool on a wire tray.

Whisk the heavy cream stiff with sugar and vanilla sugar.
Cut the cookies in halves.
Fill the bottoms with vanilla cream.
Place the other half on top.
Sprinkle powdered sugar on top of the choux pastry before serving.

Some facts about
choux pastry

When a small lump of dough consisting of flour, butter, and water finds its way from the pan, to the

baking tray, and straight into the oven, an amazing transformation is taking place. If you are lucky, the

small cookies will rise three-times in volume, and form a solid crust with a delicious cavity inside.

There's really no art to making an airy choux pastry. It all comes down to making sure you measure all of

the ingredients precisely and stir them well.

Choux pastry should be baked as soon as the dough is ready.

Make sure to keep the oven door closed during the entire baking time, otherwise the cookies will fall apart.

Choux pastry should be served as fresh as possible.

Immediately cut them in halves, this way the steam inside is emitted.

Choux pastry has a neutral flavor; you can therefore fill them with a variety of goodies.

Vanilla cream is the most common filling, but a rich berry sauce, coffee cream, ice cream,

or chocolate cream are all good alternatives.

A variety of cream cheese, mixed with caviar, shrimp, or herbs all work great as a choux pastry filling as

well. This way you can serve pastry as a starter or with a soup for dinner.

Honey cake in a roasting pan

A tasteful cake with honey, nuts, and spices that will please many mouths. The cake can last for weeks.

½ cup (100g) butter

¾ cup (250g) honey

2 eggs

½ cup (110g) sugar

2 tsp baking powder

1¾ cup (375g) all-purpose flour

1 tsp ground cinnamon

1 tsp ground cardamom

1 tsp ground ginger

½ cup (50g) chopped hazelnuts

½ cup (50g) chopped almonds

Melt butter and honey in a sauce pan. Let it cool.
Whisk eggs and sugar to an airy mixture.
Stir the honey mixture with the egg mixture.
In a separate bowl, mix flour and baking powder.
Add the dry mixture to the wet mixture.
Add spices and nuts at the end.
Preheat oven to 350°F (175°C).
Butter a roasting pan (approximately 11 inches x 14 inches)
Pour the batter into the pan.
Bake in oven for 20–25 minutes.
Cut the honey cake into squares.
Let the cake cool before serving.

Waffles

There are several recipes. My mother always added some water to the mixture to make them extra crispy.

EVERYDAY WAFFLES–10 WAFFLES

1⅓ cups (400ml) all-purpose flour

5 tbsp sugar

½ tsp ground cardamom (can be replaced with vanilla sugar).

2 cups + 2 tsp (500ml) milk

4 eggs

½ cup (100g) melted butter

Mix flour, sugar, and cardamom in a bowl.
Stir in the milk, and mix carefully in order to avoid lumps.
Stir in the eggs, one at the time.
Add butter at the end.
Let the batter swell for approximately 30 minutes.
Cook the waffles in a waffle iron.
Place the waffles on a plate with greaseproof paper in-between.

GRANDMOTHER'S SOUR CREAM WAFFLES–10 WAFFLES

3 eggs

5 tbsp sugar

½ cup (100 g) sour cream

½ tsp baking soda

1⅔ cups (400ml) milk

2 cup (500ml) flour

½ cup (100g) melted butter

Whisk eggs and sugar to an airy mixture.
Stir baking soda and sour cream; add this to the egg mixture.
Gently add milk and butter to the mixture.
Let the batter swell for approximately 30 minutes.
Cook the waffles in a waffle iron.
Place the waffles on a plate with greaseproof paper in-between.

Some facts about waffles

Waffles have a fascinating history dating back to the nineteenth century. In 1869, American Cornelius Swarthouts invented the waffle maker. Waffles even have their own official celebration. March 25th is International Waffle Day and the day celebrates both waffles and the first day of spring. Waffles are not really a cake, but I think the sweet, plaid hearts deserve some room in this book.

Sour cream waffles with strawberry jam or *brunost* are loved by both the young and old, and they are the most popular coffee dessert. You find waffles everywhere: at cafés, truck stops, chapels, and in thousands of homes.

Waffle tips

If you finish the batter long before you plan on serving your guests, you should put the batter in the fridge.

Add some water if the batter looks too thick. Water also makes the waffles extra crispy.

You will also get crispier waffles by separating the egg yolk and the egg white.

Whisk the egg whites stiff, and gently add them to the batter at the end.

Lemon cakes

Small, tempting cakes with lemon zest.

APPROXIMATELY 35 SMALL CAKES

1 cup + 3.5 tbsp (250g) butter

1 ¼ cup (250g) sugar

4 eggs

2 cups (250g) all-purpose flour

1 ½ tsp baking powder

2 lemons, organic

Melt butter. Cool.
Whisk sugar and eggs to an airy mixture.
In a separate bowl, mix flour and baking soda.
Add butter and the flour mix to the airy mixture.
Grate lemon peel.
Add this to the dough.
Add some squeezed lemon juice (a couple of tablespoons).
Blend in the lemon juice.
Preheat oven to 350°F (175°C).
Place the dough into small cupcake tins.
Bake in oven for approximately 15 minutes.
Let the cakes cool before removing them from the tins.

Tips

Use the cookie tins you have in your kitchen. I use an old cake tin with the space for 12 cookies, and as for the rest, I use classic muffin tins.
You may also cut the dough in halves and bake two small sugar cakes in buttered bread pans. They will need to bake in the oven for a little longer.
Lemon cakes served on a glass cake stand will make your dessert table look fabulous.

Norwegian blonde cookies

Thin and crispy, they are almost see-through in color. You get the round tube shape by shaping them with a wooden stick while they are still hot.

40–45 COOKIES

1 ½ cup (200g) blanched almonds

1 cup (200g) sugar

1 cup (200g) butter

2–3 tbsp all-purpose flour

½ tsp vanilla sugar

4 tbsp cream

Preheat oven to 350°F (175°C).
Chop almonds.
Put all the ingredients in a sauce pan, heat up.
Stir well.
Using a teaspoon, place the batter on a greaseproof paper.
Be aware that the cookies will rise, and make sure each cookie has enough space.
Bake in oven for 10–12 minutes, the cookies are done when they have a golden color.
Cool for a couple minutes.
Shape the cookies, using a wooden stick.
They can also be flat.
Cool the cookies on a wire rack.

Linzer Tortes

Tasteful classics bring back good memories. My mother loved bakery invitations. Her nice suit came out, and her choice was simple: Linzer Tortes with yellow vanilla cream and a cup of freshly brewed coffee.

8–10 TORTES

DOUGH:

¾ cup (185g) soft butter

⅔ cup (60g) powdered sugar

2 eggs

2¼ cups (275g) all-purpose flour

vanilla cream (recipe pg. 133)

Mix butter and powdered sugar.
Add eggs, one at a time.
Blend in flour at the end.
Stir until you have a solid dough.
Cover the dough with plastic wrap and leave it in the fridge for about an hour.
Preheat oven to 375°F (190°C).
Butter round muffin pans (approximately 3 inches).
Roll the dough out to about just under ¼ inch thick (3–4 mm).
Remember to put some of the dough aside for lids.
Cut the dough in shapes that fit the cookie tins.
Place the dough in the tins, and press gently.
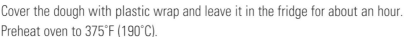
Fill the tortes with a tablespoon of vanilla cream.
Cut out lids for the cookies from the leftover dough, press the edges together as you put the lids on top of the tortes.
Bake in oven for 18–20 minutes.
Let the tortes cool before you remove them from their tins.

Did you know that…

Linzer Tortes get their name from the city Linz in Austria. This is where the famous *Linzertorte* saw the light in 1653. The recipe for Linzer Torte is said to be one of the oldest documented cake recipes.

Wasp nest

Meringue-like cookies with hints of nuts, vanilla, and chocolate. This recipe is from Western Norway, I got it from my friend's aunt, Hilda.

50–55 COOKIES

3 egg whites

1 ¼ cup (250g) sugar

2 ⅓ cup (250g) blanched almonds, chopped

2 tsp vanilla sugar

½ cup (125g) chocolate, chopped

Preheat oven to 330°F (165°C).
Beat egg whites and sugar until stiff.
Add the rest of the ingredients.
Mix until you have a soft dough.
Using a teaspoon, place the batter on a greaseproof paper.
Bake in oven for approximately 10 minutes.
Cool the cookies on a wire rack

Tips

You will need three baking pans covered with greaseproof paper for this recipe.
The cookies should be crispy on the outside and chewy on the inside.

Norwegian mud cake

The combination of dark chocolate and orange is irresistible.

½ cup (100g) butter

2 eggs

1 cup (200ml) sugar

¾ cup (150ml) all-purpose flour

1 ½ tsp vanilla sugar

Salt

5 tbsp cocoa powder

1 orange, grated rind

2 tbsp squeezed orange juice

14–16 walnuts

Preheat oven to 350°F (175°C).
Melt butter. Cool down to just above room temperature.
Mix eggs and sugar.
Add flour, vanilla sugar, a little salt, cocoa, and grated rind of orange.
Blend in butter and squeezed orange juice.
Pour the batter into a buttered Bundt pan (pan should be approximately
      9½ inches).
Bake in the middle of the oven for approximately 10 minutes.
Take the cake out of the oven and decorate with almonds.
Bake in oven for another 10 minutes.
The cake is supposed to be soft in the middle.

Tips
You may substitute orange with other sweets.
Both strawberries and raspberries go well with the chocolate cake.

Nut base cake

This nut base fits several different kinds of cakes. My favorite is nut cake with homemade applesauce, whipped cream, and chocolate sprinkles.

2 cups (300g) hazelnuts

¾ cup (150g) sugar

3 eggs

Preheat oven to 350°F (175°C).
Coarsely grind the hazelnuts.
Whisk sugar and eggs to an airy mixture.
Gently add nuts to the mixture, using a spatula.
Pour the batter in a buttered Bundt pan (approximately 9 inches).
Bake on lower rack in oven for approximately 40 minutes.
Cool the cake in the pan.

Cake decoration ideas:

* One layer with applesauce and one layer with whipped cream. Sprinkle chocolate on top.
* A mixture of vanilla cream and sour cream. Sprinkle berries on top.
* Vanilla ice cream with hot blackberry sauce.

Cookies in Jars

Cookie memories

We all want to serve something homemade with our coffee when friends unexpectedly stop by for a visit, or when we simply want to satisfy our sweet tooth cravings. Cookies in a jar are the perfect solution for this.

They are easy to bake, and they can be stored for weeks. Furthermore, they are cherished when brought along on a family hiking trip.

During the summer, time is typically spent outside rather than inside the kitchen. Cookies in a jar bring back good memories. My mother usually baked oatcakes and oat crisps before we went to our summer cabin.

The cookies were gently placed in jars with greaseproof paper, and the temptations were always kept safely on the top shelf. Underneath, small and eager children's hands were kept out of reach.

The tradition of cookies in a jar varies from country to country. I got to experience this myself one Sunday morning in the Netherlands, where I lived back in the day. We were invited for coffee at my friends' place. The hostess was pouring freshly brewed coffee in rose-patterned coffee cups, and the cookie jar was passed along the table. Modestly, I picked out one cookie (other people took cookies as well) and I expected the cookie jar to return later . . . but it never did. As soon as the cookie jar had been passed around the table it was quickly put back on the kitchen shelf.

Traditions vary, but the sparse behavior came as a shock for someone like me, who was used to sumptuous, Norwegian dessert tables.

Tea bread

This recipe is good and old. You may want to double the recipe as the cookies have a tendency to disappear quickly.

30–35 COOKIES

1⅔ cups (400ml) all-purpose flour

½ cup (100g) butter

½ cup (100ml) sugar

½ tsp baker's ammonia

2 eggs (put some aside to brush the cookies)

Almond flakes and pearl sugar for decoration

Preheat oven to 390°F (200°C).
Rub flour and butter together in a bowl.
Mix in sugar and baker's ammonia.
Lightly whisk eggs, put some aside for brushing the cookies later.
Add eggs. Gently rub the dough, using your fingers, until you have a
    smooth dough.
Cut the dough in three parts and roll them to similar lengths to fit the baking
    tray.
Place the lengths on a baking tray covered with greaseproof paper.
Press the lengths gently, using your hands.
Brush the lengths with the egg you set aside.
Sprinkle with almond flakes and pearl sugar.
Bake in oven for approximately 15 minutes.
Cut the cookies diagonally while they are still hot.
Cool on a wire rack.

Tips
Allow the cookies to cool completely before putting them in a jar with
greaseproof paper covering the bottom.

Oatmeal cookies

A classic at our house. Oatmeal cookies with brunost taste extra good with a freshly brewed cup of coffee.

1 cup (500ml) oatmeal

1 cup (200ml) milk

½ cup (125g) butter, melted

1 cup (200ml) all-purpose flour

1 tsp baking powder

½ tsp salt

1 tbsp sugar

Preheat oven to 390°F (200°C).
Warm up milk, let the oatmeal swell in it for about 10 minutes.
Add melted butter and stir.
In a separate bowl, mix flour and baking powder, then add salt and
sugar.
Mix all the wet and dry ingredients together gently until you have
a smooth dough.
Roll out the dough into a circle, approximately ¼ inch (½ cm) thick.
Use a round cookie cutter on the dough, approximately 2½–3
inches (7 cm).
Put the cookies on a greaseproof baking sheet, you will need two
baking sheets for this recipe.
Gently press the cookies using fork tines or a cookie press.
Bake on the middle rack of the oven for 15–18 minutes.
Cool on a wire rack.

Tips

Instead of using cookie cutters to shape the cookies, you may use
a round glass.

Oatmeal macaroons

Old fashioned cookies. Simple to make, wonderful in taste.

20 COOKIES

½ cup (100g) butter

1 cup (200ml) all-purpose flour

1 tsp baking powder

½ cup (300ml) oatmeal

¼ cup (50ml) sugar

¼ cup (50ml) water

Preheat oven to 390°F (200°C).
Melt butter.
In a separate bowl, mix flour and baking powder.
Add oatmeal and sugar.
Pour butter and water in the mixture, gently mix all the ingredients.
Place the cookies, using a spoon, on a greased baking tray.
Bake in the middle of the oven for approximately 15 minutes.
Cool on a wire rack.

Tips

With a few, simple adjustments oatmeal macaroons can turn into chocolate cookies, perfect snacks with a cup of coffee.
Dip a freshly baked cookie in melted chocolate so that half of it is covered in chocolate.
Cool the cookies in a fridge to harden up the chocolate before you serve them.

Oatmeal cookies with currants

Cookies filled with oatmeal and small currants.

APPROXIMATELY 40 COOKIES

1 cup (200g) butter

1 cup (200ml) sugar

1 ¼ cup (300ml) all-purpose flour

1 tsp baking powder

½ cup (300ml) oatmeal

½ cup (100ml) currants

Preheat oven to 350°F (175°C).

Stir butter and sugar well together.

In a separate bowl, mix flour and baking powder.

Blend all the ingredients together until you have a smooth dough.

Cut the dough into 40 pieces.

Roll the pieces into small balls and put them on a pan covered with greaseproof paper
(you will need two pans for this recipe).

Gently press the cookies with a fork.

Bake on the middle rack of the oven for 18–20 minutes.

Cool on a wire rack.

Almond crisps

With tastes of almonds and vanilla, these cookies are similar to the classic Italian biscotti.

APPROXIMATELY 30 COOKIES

½ cup (100g) butter

⅔ cup (150ml) sugar

1 egg

1⅔ cups (400ml) all-purpose flour

1 tsp baking powder

1 tsp vanilla sugar

¾ cup (70g) almonds, shredded

Preheat oven to 350°F (175°C).
Stir butter and sugar to an airy and porous mixture.
Add the egg.
In a separate bowl, mix flour, baking powder, vanilla sugar, and almonds.
Gently blend all the ingredients to a smooth dough.
Divide the dough into three pieces.
Roll the pieces into lengths of approximately 12 inches each.
Place the lengths on a pan covered with greaseproof paper.
Gently press the lengths, using your hands.
Bake on the middle rack of the oven for approximately 20 minutes.
Take the lengths out of the oven and let them rest for 5 minutes.
Cut the lengths diagonally.
Place the cookies back on the baking tray.
Bake in oven for another 15–20 minutes.

Tips

You can add a variety of different spices to this basic recipe such as cardamom, cinnamon, or lavender.
The cookies taste extra good if you add chocolate chips.

Almond cookies

Light, airy cookies. Quick and easy to make; a perfect gift to give a hostess. Put the almond cookies in a jar or a cellophane bag and tie with a bow the next time you are invited over to a friend's house.

APPROXIMATELY 40 COOKIES

1 cup (200g) soft butter

¾ cup (140g) sugar

⅓ cup (50g) almonds

1 egg

1 cup + 2 tbsp (150g) all-purpose flour

½ cup (125g) potato flour

1 tsp baker's ammonia

Preheat oven to 355°F (180°C).
Stir butter and sugar to an airy mixture.
Add almonds and mix in the egg.
In a separate bowl, mix flour, potato flour, and baker's ammonia.
Gently blend all the ingredients to a smooth dough.
Divide the dough into four pieces.
Roll the pieces into lengths and cut each length into ten small pieces.
Roll each piece into balls and put them on two pans covered with greaseproof
    paper.
Gently press the cookies, using your hands.
Bake on the middle rack of the oven for approximately 15 minutes.
Cool on a wire rack.

Tips

Keep in mind that cookies tend to flatten while baking in the oven.
Calculate good distance between each cookie.
The cookies are best stored in containers with air proof lids.

Chocolate biscuits

A small dessert for the afternoon coffee.

25–30 COOKIES

½ cup (100g) soft butter

½ cup (100g) sugar

2 cups (250g) all-purpose flour

1 tsp baking powder

4 tbsp cocoa

1 tsp vanilla sugar

1 egg

DECORATION:

1 egg

Pearl sugar

Preheat oven to 355°F (180°C).
Stir butter and sugar to an airy mixture.
In a separate bowl, mix flour and baking powder.
Add cocoa and vanilla sugar.
Blend all the ingredients to a smooth dough; add the egg at the end.
Divide the dough into three pieces and roll them into lengths.
Place the lengths on a pan covered with greaseproof paper.
Gently use a rolling pin over the lengths, using a roller pan.
Whisk an egg, brush the lengths and sprinkle over with pearl sugar.
Gently use the roller again to make sure the pearl sugar is stuck.
Bake on the middle rack in oven for 12–15 minutes.
Let the lengths cool for a couple minutes then cut the chocolate bis-
cuits diagonally.
Cool on a wire rack.

Did you know . . .

Pearl sugar is merely sugar crystals that have been cooked extra long.
They remain whole and white, even after being baked in the oven.
Pearl sugar is perfect as decoration for cakes and biscuits.

Chocolate half moons

Cookies with a taste of chocolate and orange.

20 COOKIES

½ cup (100g) soft butter

½ cup (100ml) sugar

1¼ cup (300ml) all-purpose flour

1 tsp baker's ammonia

3 cup (40g) potato flour

1 tsp vanilla sugar

3 tbsp freshly squeezed orange juice

2 ounces (50g) chocolate

Preheat oven to 400°F (200°C).
Stir butter and sugar to an airy mixture.
In a separate bowl, mix flour, baker's ammonia, potato flour,
    and vanilla sugar.
Blend the dry and the wet mixture together and add orange juice.
Stir until you have a smooth dough.
Cut the dough in halves; roll out two lengths.
Divide each length into ten pieces.
Shape the pieces into round cookies; put them on a baking tray
    covered with greaseproof paper.
Press each cookie gently, using your hand.
Bake in oven for 12–14 minutes.
Cool on a wire rack.
Melt chocolate over a bowl of hot water.
Dip the cookies in chocolate, half of them will be covered in
    chocolate.
Cool on greaseproof paper in a cold room.

Tips

If you double the recipe, you may want to dip half of the cookies
in chocolate and leave the other half plain.
You may also add some organic orange zest to the dough.
Do not cool the cookies in the fridge; the cookies will turn grey
and lose some of their taste.

Spice cookies

Crispy cookies with a taste of cardamom, ginger, and cinnamon.

APPROXIMATELY 30 COOKIES

1 cup + 2 tbsp (140g) all-purpose flour

2 tbsp potato flour or cornstarch

½ cup (60g) powdered sugar

½ tsp ground cardamom

½ tsp ground ginger

½ tsp ground cinnamon

½ cup (100g) soft butter

1 egg yolk (put the egg white aside for brushing)

DECORATION:

Sugar and ground cinnamon

Mix flour, potato flour, and powdered sugar in a mixing bowl.

Add spices and butter.

Add the egg yolk at the end and blend until you have a smooth dough.

Cover the bowl with plastic wrap and store in a fridge for approximately 30 minutes.

Preheat oven to 350°F (175°C).

Remove the dough from the bowl; cut it into three pieces.

Roll the pieces into lengths (approximately the same length as the baking tray).

Brush the lengths with egg white.

Sprinkle with sugar and cinnamon.

Cut the lengths into little cookies and place them on a baking tray covered with greaseproof paper.

Bake for approximately 15 minutes.

Cool on a wire rack.

Tips

In this recipe you can use spices of your own preference.
You may also sprinkle with chopped nuts.

Krumkake

Krumkake is a Norwegian waffle cookie served traditionally around Christmastime. But I think it's a great idea to surprise someone with krumkake in the middle of summer, served with whipped cream and the season's berries. To make these cookies a Norwegian krumkake iron is needed, a pizzelle iron would work as well. These are available at most culinary or home-goods stores.

3 medium-sized eggs

¾ cup (170g) sugar

¾ cup (170g) butter, melted

2 tbsp water

2–3 drops almond extract

1⅓ cup (170g) all-purpose flour

Whisk eggs and sugar to an airy mixture.
Add melted butter, water, and almond extract.
Blend in flour; stir until you have a smooth dough.
Cover the mixing bowl and store overnight in a fridge.
Keep in mind that the dough needs to be brought to room temperature before you bake it in the oven.
Butter a heated krumkake iron.
Pour approximately 1 tablespoon of batter, smear it and bake.
Roll the cake immediately after it is done baking.
Cool on a wire rack.

Tips

It is important to make the krumkake dough the night before baking.
Use thin cotton gloves when you roll the cake to avoid being burnt.
You may make classic krumkake á la cones or place the hot krumkake in a cup. If you decide to put it in a cup, the krumkake tastes delicious when served with whipped cream or other creams with berries.
Store the krumkake in cake tins, layered with thin sheets of paper in between the cookies.

Why do cakes fail?

IF THE CAKE FAILS TO RISE:

Too short stirring time.

Too much flour.

Not enough baking powder.

The batter is stirred for too long after flour and other dry ingredients have been added.

The oven door is opened too early, or too often during the baking time.

IF THE CAKE IS RISING OVER THE EDGES OF THE PAN:

The oven is too cold.

Pan is too small.

Pan is over-filled (the batter should always cover two-thirds of the pan).

Too much baking powder.

IF THE CAKE BREAKS:

Too hot oven.

Flour and baking powder has not been mixed well enough before being added

to the rest of the mixture.

Too much flour.

The oven's underheat is too strong.

IF THE CAKE FALLS IN THE MIDDLE:

Not enough baking time.

Too high temperature in oven.

The oven's underheat is too strong.

IF THE DOUGH IS TOO STICKY:

Not enough fat, or pan is not evenly buttered.

The cake has not rested enough before it has been removed from the pan.

Cake accompaniments

Now and then, a heavy vanilla cream, hot chocolate sauce, some ice cream, or a sauce of the season's berries will give the cake a little something extra.

Custard

1 vanilla bean

1 cup (250ml) milk

3 tbsp sugar

2 tbsp cornstarch

4 egg yolks

½ cup heavy cream

Cut the vanilla bean in half along the middle. Scrape out the seeds.
Heat up milk with vanilla seeds until it starts to boil.
Whisk egg yolks with sugar and cornstarch to an airy mixture.
Pour this into the warm milk mixture while you stir until it thickens; keep the pan on middle-heat.
Pour the sauce into a bowl and cover with plastic wrap.
Cool the vanilla sauce in the fridge.
Whisk heavy cream lightly, mix it with the vanilla sauce when you are ready to serve,
Vanilla sauce will remain fresh for 3–4 days as long as you store it in an airtight container in the fridge.

Vanilla cream

1 vanilla bean

2 cups (500ml) milk

5 egg yolks

½ cup (100ml) sugar

2 tbsp corsnstarch

1 cup (200ml) heavy cream

Cut the vanilla bean in half along the middle.
Scrape out the seeds.
Pour milk in a sauce pan, add vanilla seeds.
Slowly boil, stirring well.
Remove the pan from the hot plate.
Whisk egg yolks, sugar, and cornstarch.
Add this to the milk mixture.
Carefully, boil up until the cream thickens.
Constantly stir vigorously.
Let the cream cool.

Homemade vanilla ice cream

1 vanilla bean

5 egg yolks

½ cup (100g) sugar

1 ½ cup (300ml) heavy cream

Cut the vanilla bean in halves along the middle, scrape out the seeds.
Whisk egg yolks and sugar to an airy mixture.
Add vanilla seeds.
Whisk the cream until you get a thick cream.
Gently mix the heavy cream with the mixture.
Pour the ice cream into a plastic box; put the box in the freezer.
Stir the ice cream a few times until it is frozen.

Chocolate sauce

3½ tbsp (50g) butter

½ cup (100g) sugar

1 cup (200ml) whipped cream

3½ ounces (100g) dark chocolate

Put butter, sugar, and whipped cream in a sauce pan.
Stir vigorously until it is boiling.
Let the mixture simmer for a couple of minutes while you stir.
Remove the pan from the heat, stir until the sauce has cooled a little.
Cut the chocolate into pieces.
Stir while you add chocolate into the mixture.
The sauce is ready when it is thick and shiny.

A simpler way to make chocolate sauce is to mix little pieces of
chocolate with 1½ cup (300ml) of whipped cream. Let the mixture
simmer on low temperature while you stir until it thickens.

Chocolate cream

1 cup (125g) soft butter

1 cup (125g) powdered sugar

1 egg yolk

4 tbsp cocoa

Whisk butter and powdered sugar.
Add the egg yolk and cocoa.
Stir well until you have a smooth cream.

Berry sauce

1½ cup (200g) berries (raspberries, blueberries,
  or strawberries)

1 cup (200ml) water

3 tbsp sugar

Boil water and berries in a sauce pan.
Add sugar.
Stir vigorously until the sugar is dissolved.
Smooth the mixture with a blender.

You may also make a simpler berry sauce by mixing
fresh or frozen berries in a electric mixer. Sweeten
the sauce by adding sugar or powdered sugar.

Recipe index

THANK YOU

To my partner Gunnar who has tasted all of the cookies and given them his blessings (he may have gained a few pounds along the way).

To my publishing editor in Norway, Inger Margrethe Karlsen. Her enthusiasm has always given me determination and extra energy.

To designer Lise Mosveen for your positivity and aesthetic sense of design.
To my mother who always baked such amazing sweets.

Photography: Kari Finngaard
Graphic design: Lise Mosveen

Skyhorse Publishing books may be purchased in bulk at special discounts for sales promotion, corporate gifts, fund-raising, or educational purposes. Special editions can also be created to specifications. For details, contact the Special Sales Department, Skyhorse Publishing, 307 West 36th Street, 11th Floor, New York, NY 10018 or info@skyhorsepublishing.com.

Skyhorse® and Skyhorse Publishing® are registered trademarks of Skyhorse Publishing, Inc.®, a Delaware corporation.

www.skyhorsepublishing.com

10 9 8 7 6 5 4 3 2 1
Library of Congress Cataloging-in-Publication Data is available on file.

Cover design by Sarah Brody
Cover photographs: Kari Finngaard

Print ISBN: 978-1-63450-398-3
Ebook ISBN: 978-1-63450-878-0

Printed in China